Le Cordon Bleu

Techniques and Recipes

Fish & Shellfish

LE CORDON BLEU

TECHNIQUES AND RECIPES
FISH &
SHELLFISH

JENI WRIGHT AND ERIC TREUILLE

CASSELL

A CASSELL BOOK

This edition first published in the United Kingdom in 1998 by
Cassell plc
Wellington House
125 Strand
London WC2R 0BB

Created and produced by
CARROLL & BROWN LIMITED
20 Lonsdale Road
London NW6 6RD

Material in this book has been previously published in
Le Cordon Bleu Complete Cooking Techniques
published by Cassell at £25

British Library Catalogue-in-Publication Data
A catalogue record for this book is available from the
British Library

ISBN 0-304-35121-0

Reproduced by Colourscan, Singapore
Printed and bound in Great Britain by Jarrold Book Printing,
Thetford, Norfolk

CONTENTS

CHOOSING FRESH SEAFOOD

Seafood falls into four categories: seawater, freshwater, preserved fish (smoked, salted and dried) and shellfish. All but preserved fish should be eaten as fresh as possible. It is only really possible to judge the freshness of a whole fish; fillets, steaks and pieces are more difficult to assess. Freshwater fish should smell fresh and clean, while marine fish should smell of the sea.

EYES should be full, moist, bright and bulging. Avoid fish with dull, dry, shrivelled or sunken eyes

GILLS should be clean, red and bright, with no signs of greying or traces of slime

BODY should be firm, smooth and quite stiff, not limp, floppy or lumpy

BUYING FILLETS AND STEAKS

It is better to buy fillets or steaks that are cut from the whole fish while you wait, rather than pre-cut, or to buy the fish and cut or fillet it yourself (see pages 13 and 15). Very large fish, such as monkfish, shark, tuna and large cod, are almost always sold ready prepared. When judging the freshness of fillets and steaks, the smell and texture of the fish can be used as a guide. The fish should smell fresh (smelling of the sea in marine fish) and look moist, firm and springy, not dry.

HANDLING SEAFOOD

Fish and shellfish deteriorate much more quickly than meat, so they must be cooked on the day of purchase or as soon as possible afterwards.

Oily fish such as mackerel, herring and salmon, spoil more quickly than white fish because their natural oils turn rancid. If seafood has to be stored overnight, wrap it in damp cloths and keep it in the coldest part of the refrigerator. Whole fish will keep longer if gutted first.

BUYING SHELLFISH

LOBSTERS AND CRABS If you are buying live, choose an active specimen that feels heavy for its size. If buying cooked, check that the shell is undamaged and the claws intact. The smell should be fresh and not strong.

MUSSELS, CLAMS AND COCKLES Avoid those that are excessively covered in mud or barnacles, or that appear to be cracked or damaged. Discard any that remain open when tapped.

SCALLOPS These are most often sold opened, cleaned and trimmed rather than in their closed shells. Check that they smell sweet; if so, they are fresh. The flesh of fresh scallops is slightly grey and translucent, not perfectly white.

OYSTERS The shells must be undamaged and tightly closed. When tapped they should sound solid. Traditionally, they were picked when there was an "r" in the month to avoid infection during warm weather. They are now generally sold all year round because of modern techniques of oyster farming and improved methods of transport.

PRAWNS These are sold in several ways: cooked in or out of their shells, or raw in their shells. Cooked prawns should be bright pink and firm, not watery. Raw prawns should also be firm, with shiny grey shells. Avoid any prawns with black spots – a sure sign of ageing.

SKIN should be shiny and damp to the touch, not dry or dull. Any natural markings and colouring should be undimmed. For example, red mullet and snapper should be a bright pinky red; trout, herring and mackerel should be irridescent; salmon a shimmering silver; and parrot fish a brilliant blue

UNUSUAL FISH

There are many exotic fish on sale at large supermarkets and city fishmongers, many of them beautifully marked with spectacular, irridescent colours.

- Emperor Fish, also called *capitaine rouge*, *capitaine blanc* and *lascar*, has a strong flavour and is quite bony. Bake whole.
- Gurnard is tasty and firm fleshed, good in fish stews and soups.

- Sea Bream has sweet, firm flesh and is inexpensive. Gilt-head bream – *daurade* in French – is especially good. Bake whole with or without stuffing.
- Shark steaks are meaty and firm with very little bone. Good for chargrilling and in stews.
- Tilapia has firm white flesh and good flavour. It can be steamed, baked, grilled or barbecued, whole or in fillets.

USING FISH & SHELLFISH

Fish and shellfish are delicate foods to cook – they have fragile flesh that requires careful handling. Choose the freshest you can, and make sure they are thoroughly cleaned before use. Cook fish just long enough to set the protein and turn the flesh opaque; if overcooked, fish will become tough and dry. When substituting one fish for another, make sure it is of a similar structure, texture and flavour.

ROUND FISH

This variable family runs the gamut in size and shape. Their flesh is typically firm and "meaty" tasting, meaning they pair well with other assertive ingredients.

FISH	COOKING METHODS
BASS/ MULLET	Poach, steam, bake, barbecue
BREAM	Bake, braise
CATFISH	Stew, braise, grill
COD/HADDOCK	Pan-fry, deep-fry, grill, poach, bake
DOGFISH	Bake, stew, grill
EEL	Bake, stew, grill
HAKE	Bake wrapped, steam, pan-fry
MACKEREL	Pan-fry, grill, barbecue
MONKFISH	Pan-fry, bake, grill, barbecue
SALMON/TROUT	Pan-fry, poach, steam, bake, grill, barbecue
SARDINES	Grill, barbecue, pan-fry, bake
SNAPPER/MAHI MAHI/ ORANGE ROUGH	Poach, pan-fry, grill, barbecue, bake
SWORDFISH/TUNA/ SHARK	Grill, barbecue, pan-fry, bake, stew, braise

FLAT FISH

To showcase the subtle flavour of these fine-textured varieties, choose for preference a swift cooking process that uses as few other ingredients as possible. Braising works particularly well because this moist-heat method tends to concentrate the natural, and often very delicate, flavour of the fish.

FISH	COOKING METHODS
BRILL	Bake wrapped and unwrapped, steam, poach, grill, pan-fry
GROUPER	Bake wrapped and unwrapped, steam, poach, grill, pan-fry
HALIBUT	Poach, pan-fry, braise
JOHN DORY	Poach, grill, pan-fry
PLAICE	Pan-fry, deep-fry, poach, steam, grill, bake
RAY/SKATE	Pan-fry, bake
SOLE	Grill, pan-fry, deep-fry, steam, bake
TURBOT	Bake wrapped and unwrapped, steam, poach, grill, pan-fry

SHELLFISH

Some molluscs require special attention. A live shellfish yields the best flavour, so store mussels or clams in salted water (4 tbsp salt to 1 litre water) not fresh water, which will kill them. Bearding mussels more than a few hours before cooking can spoil them.

SHELLFISH	WHAT TO LOOK FOR	COOKING METHODS
CLAMS/COCKLES	*Shells should be tightly closed, not chipped or broken* *Shucked clams should be plump and smell fresh throughout*	Steam – in shell Grill, bake – half shell Stew, pan-fry – shucked
CRAB	*Active and heavy* *Shell undamaged and claws intact*	Boil, steam
LOBSTER	*Heavy for size* *Tail curled under* *Claws intact and undamaged*	Boil, steam – in shell Grill – split
MUSSELS	*Shells tightly shut and undamaged* *Not light and loose when shaken*	Boil, steam – in shell Grill, bake – half shell Pan-fry, stew – shucked
OYSTERS	*Shells tightly closed and undamaged* *Shucked oysters should be plump and uniform in size with clear liquid*	Serve raw Bake, grill – half shell Pan-fry, stew – shucked
PRAWNS	*Firm meat that feels full in the shell* *Moist appearance and fresh smell* *Avoid any that smell of chlorine or have black spots on the shell*	Pan-fry, deep-fry, stir-fry, grill, barbecue, bake, poach, steam
SCALLOPS	*Free of liquid with a sweet fresh odour whether on half shell or shucked* *Check the body section is plump and creamy white* *Coral pink and moist* *Avoid any with a sulphurous smell*	Bake, grill – half shell Poach, pan-fry – shucked
SQUID/ OCTOPUS	*Clear eyes, fresh smell* *White moist flesh*	Deep-fry, pan-fry, poach, bake, stew
WHELKS/ WINKLES	*Should smell sweet* *Move into shell when prodded* *Lid should be moist and firmly in place*	Boil – in shell Stew – shelled

FISH ON THE MENU

From coast to coast, great cooks pair their region's catch with local ingredients and cooking techniques to create internationally appealing dishes.

FRANCE – *Bouillabaisse* (a lusty fish stew of Mediterranean fish and shellfish with saffron and fennel) originated in Marseille.
GREECE – *Kalamari* (squid deep-fried in a light batter and served with lemon wedges and chilled retsina) is a favourite midday snack on the Aegean.
ITALY – *Spaghetti alle vongole* (with clam sauce) is a staple in trattorias throughout Italy.
MEXICO – *Ceviche* (raw fish "cooked" not by heat, but by the acidity of lime juice) is refreshing with a tart tang.
SPAIN – *Paella* (shellfish and squid with saffron rice, tomatoes and garlic) is a favourite festive dish.
UNITED STATES – *New England Clam Chowder* (a soup made with potatoes, clams and cream) dates back to the early 1700s. *Manhattan Clam Chowder* (a spicy tomato- and clam-based soup) came to fame later, in the 1930s.

PREPARING WHOLE ROUND FISH

Round fish are so named for their body shape – a round belly as opposed to a flat one, with an eye on either side of the head. Popular varieties include trout and salmon. Round fish yield two fillets, one from each side of the backbone. Though most often gutted before being sold, round fish can be cleaned at home if you like. Once gutted, round fish can be boned and stuffed or filleted.

TRIMMING AND SCALING

Most fish, such as the salmon pictured here, have scales that need to be removed before cooking. Removing scales is a simple but messy task, so work as near to the sink as possible. Trimming any fins beforehand will make scaling more straightforward and, because some fins are spiny, will be gentler on your hands and make the fish easier to handle. Trim the fins with a pair of kitchen scissors but use a large chef's knife to remove the scales. Fish scalers are also available from specialist kitchen shops.

1 Cut off the three fins that run along the stomach of the fish from the head to the tail – the pectoral, ventral and anal fins – with kitchen scissors.

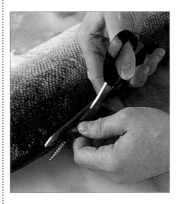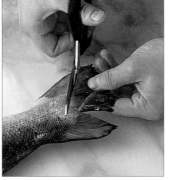

2 Turn the fish over and cut off the dorsal fins that run along the back of the fish with the kitchen scissors. It is important to cut off the fins as they harbour bacteria.

3 For fish that are to be served whole, you can make the tail look more attractive by cutting it into a neat "V" shape (see box, left) with kitchen scissors.

4 Hold the tail of the fish firmly. Scrape the scales off the fish with the back of a large chef's knife, working from the tail to the head. Rinse the fish thoroughly.

GUTTING THROUGH THE GILLS

Round fish that are to be served with their heads on should have their internal organs (innards) removed through their gills. This method retains their shape, ensuring a neat presentation. The fish can then be stuffed or left unstuffed. If the latter, bone the fish along its backbone (see page 13).

1 Locate and lift up the gill flap behind the head of the fish and cut out the gills with kitchen scissors. Discard the gills.

SCORING

Today's chefs dress up plain grilled, barbecued or steamed fish by making cuts in the flesh and inserting sprigs of herbs. Slices of garlic can also be inserted or, for an Asian dish, lemon grass, spring onions and fresh root ginger can be used. The flavours of the herbs penetrate the fish flesh during cooking.

2 Hold the fish belly up. Make a small cut at the bottom of the stomach and insert the points of the scissors or your fingers through it. Cut through the innards to loosen them from the fish.

3 Insert your fingers inside the gill opening. Grasp hold of the innards and pull them out. Check the hole cut at the bottom of the stomach, making sure no organs remain. Discard the innards.

4 Hold the fish under cold running water and let the water run through the inside of the fish from the gill opening to the tail. Rinse until the water runs clear. Pat dry with paper towels.

Make 2–3 slashes in one side of the fish, cutting through to the bones. Turn the fish over and repeat on the other side. Tuck the seasonings into the slashes. The fish is now ready for cooking.

GUTTING THROUGH THE STOMACH

The easiest and most common way to remove the innards from a fish is through its stomach. Use this method for fish that are to be served whole, stuffed or unstuffed, and where a pristine shape is not required, particularly if the fish is to be boned before or after cooking.

1 Cut out the gills behind the head and discard. Make a small cut at the bottom of the stomach, then cut along the underside, stopping just below the gills.

2 With your hand, grasp hold of the innards and pull them out. Discard the innards; they are not suitable for the stockpot.

3 Run along each side of the backbone with a tablespoon. This removes any blood vessels which detract from the fish's appearance and can make it taste bitter when cooked. Rinse the fish under cold running water, then pat dry with paper towels. The fish is now ready for cooking.

11

BONING SMALL ROUND FISH

Small, oily fish, such as the sardine shown here, have such soft bones that they can be boned with your fingers rather than a knife.

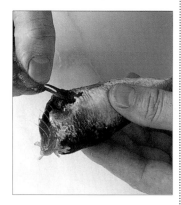

1 With your fingertips, break off the head of the fish behind the gills. Discard the head and gills. Insert your forefinger into the head end of the fish and run it down the belly so that it slits open. Working from head to tail, pull out the innards and discard them.

2 Open the fish out and, working from head to tail again, pull out the backbone. Release the backbone at the tail end by snapping it off with your fingers. Rinse the fish thoroughly and pat dry with paper towels. The fish is now ready for cooking.

BONING THROUGH THE STOMACH

Once the innards have been removed through the opening in the stomach of the fish (see page 11), you should also remove the backbone through the stomach. Gutting and boning a fish through its stomach, as with the salmon shown here, creates a natural cavity for stuffings.

1 Hold the fish on its back and use a filleting knife to cut upwards between the rib bones and the flesh on one side of the backbone so that the rib bones are loosened.

2 Slide the blade of the knife down the rib bones close to the backbone so that all the ribs on this side are detached from the flesh. Repeat from step 1 to free the ribs from the other side of the flesh.

3 Cut the backbone from the fish with a pair of kitchen scissors, and discard along with the ribs.

4 Remove the fine pin bones from both sides of the fish's spine with a pair of tweezers. Run your fingers from the head to the tail, again on both sides, feeling for pin bones you may have overlooked. Wipe the fish dry with paper towels. The fish is now ready for cooking.

BONING ALONG THE BACKBONE

To preserve the shape of a whole round fish, leaving the stomach cavity intact for stuffing, bone it along the back. The fish, such as the trout shown here, should be gutted through the gills.

1 Working from the tail to the head, cut along each side of the backbone with a pair of kitchen scissors.

2 Carefully detach the backbone at both the head and tail ends of the fish, using a chef's knife. Lift out the backbone and discard. Wipe the fish thoroughly dry with paper towels. The fish is now ready for cooking.

FILLETING ROUND FISH

Once a fish has been scaled, trimmed and gutted through the stomach (see page 11), it can be filleted or cut into large boneless slices. Two fillets – one from each side – can be cut from round fish, such as the salmon shown here. Use a sharp, flexible filleting knife and work carefully to leave as little flesh on the bones as possible. Check the fillets for pin bones (see page 12).

1 Make a cut around the back of the head then, working from head to tail, using the rib bones as a guide, cut along one side of the backbone. Holding the knife flat use long, even strokes to cut the flesh away. Run the knife over the rib bones, holding the free flesh with the other hand.

2 Turn the fish over and repeat step 1 to remove the remaining fillet. The head and carcass will be left. Use the bones along with the head, but not the gills, to make fish stock, if you like. The fillets may be skinned as for flat fish (see page 15) before cooking, depending on what the finished dish calls for.

BONING MONKFISH

If you buy monkfish on the bone you will need to know how to remove the bone if a recipe calls for fillets.

1 Lay the monkfish down, grasp hold of the skin and pull it back towards the tail of the fish.

2 Cut along both sides of the backbone with a chef's knife, separating the flesh of the fish into two fillets. The backbone can then be used to make fish stock.

3 Carefully remove the dark membrane from the underside of each fillet. Wipe the fillets thoroughly with paper towels. They are now ready for cooking.

PREPARING WHOLE FLAT FISH

Flat fish are so named because they are flat-shaped. Popular varieties include plaice, sole, turbot and brill. Flat fish swim on their sides and have both eyes on their top side, or back, which is dark for camouflage. The underneath of flat fish is white. In order to preserve their shape, flat fish are always gutted, from behind the head and gills. Because gutting is done at sea, they are invariably sold ready-gutted.

SCALING

You will need to remove the scales from the skin of the fish if you are planning to serve the fish whole or if you have bought a fish that is not already scaled by the fishmonger.

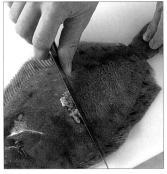

This is a messy job, best done near the sink. Lay the fish dark-side up and hold the tail firmly. Working from tail to head with the back of a chef's knife, scrape the scales off the fish. Hold the fish by the tail under the cold tap and rinse it thoroughly, washing away the scales by rubbing the skin vigorously with your hands.

SKINNING

If you are serving a flat fish whole, only the dark skin needs to be removed – the white skin is left on to help hold the fish together during cooking. If you plan to serve the fish as fillets, you can remove both dark and white skins while the fish is whole, as with this Dover sole, or you can skin individual fillets.

1 Working on the dark side first, scrape the skin away from the tail with a knife to loosen it from the flesh.

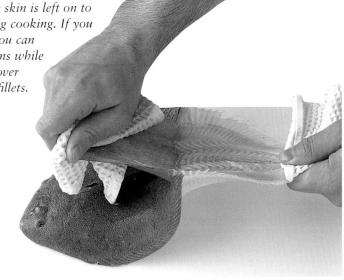

2 Grasp the skin and tail using a tea towel to prevent your hands from slipping. Pull the skin away from the tail and over the head, detaching it completely from the fish.

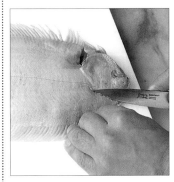

3 Turn the fish white-side up. Cut around the head of the fish to loosen the skin.

4 Working from head to tail on both sides, use your fingers to loosen the skin and pull it back from around the edge of the fish. Once the skin is well loosened, grasp it at the tail end and pull it away from the flesh, detaching it completely.

FILLETING

Depending on its size, a flat fish yields two or four fillets. Whether you are going to skin the fillets or not, you should always trim and scale the fish before filleting. Here a large brill is separated into four fillets.

1 Lay the fish dark-side up on a cutting board. Cut around the outside of the fish with a filleting knife where the flesh meets the fins, carefully tracing the shape of the fillets.

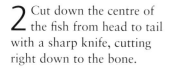

2 Cut down the centre of the fish from head to tail with a sharp knife, cutting right down to the bone.

3 Working from the centre of the fish to the edge, cut away one fillet with long, broad strokes of the knife. Take care to leave as little flesh still on the bones as possible. Turn the fish around and remove the second fillet in the same way.

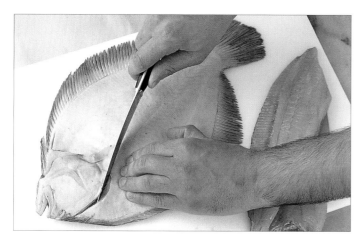

4 Turn the fish over. Make a cut around the back of the head and around the outside edge of the flesh. Cut down to the bone along the centre of the fish, working from head to tail. Follow step 3 to remove the two remaining fillets.

SKINNING A FISH FILLET

Even when bought packaged from the supermarket, fish fillets most often come with their skins on – which helps them to maintain their shape. The technique of skinning a fish fillet is important; if the skin and the flesh are not separated properly, the flesh may come away with the skin or be ragged and torn.

Lay the fillet skin-side down and make a cut across the flesh at the tail end. Dip your fingertips in salt to help you get a good grip, grasp the tail end and insert the knife in the cut. Working away from you and using a sawing action, hold the knife at a shallow angle. Move the knife between the flesh and skin until you reach the other end of the fillet.

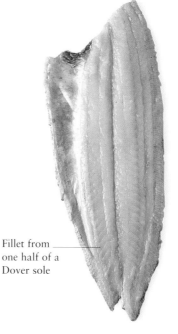

Fillet from one half of a Dover sole

Fillets cut lengthwise in half for paupiettes

Sichuan Fish

A Chinese classic, your choice of a whole, firm-fleshed fish such as red snapper, sea bass or grey mullet, is deep-fried in a wok, then braised in an aromatic sauce flavoured with garlic, ginger and chilli.

SERVES 4

1 whole fish,
weighing about 1 kg

Salt

500 ml groundnut oil

1 tsp cornflour

2–4 garlic cloves, shredded

2.5 cm piece of fresh root
ginger, peeled and cut into
very fine shreds

2 tbsp Shaoxing rice wine or
dry sherry

1–3 tbsp chilli bean sauce

2 tbsp light soy sauce

150 ml fish stock or water

2 spring onions, cut into very
fine shreds

2 fresh red chillies, deseeded
and cut into julienne

1 tsp caster sugar

1 tsp Oriental sesame oil

Fresh coriander sprigs,
to garnish

Prepare the fish and remove any scales if necessary. Score both sides of the fish with three diagonal cuts, spacing them evenly along its length. Sprinkle the fish with salt on both sides.

Heat a wok over a high heat until it is hot, then slowly pour in the oil down the side. When the oil is very hot, carefully add the fish and deep-fry, turning once until golden brown on both sides, about 4 minutes.

Carefully remove the fish with two fish slices and allow to drain on paper towels. Pour off the hot oil, leaving about 1 tbsp.

Mix the cornflour to a paste with 2 tsp water; set aside. Add the garlic and ginger to the hot wok and stir-fry briefly, then add the rice wine, chilli bean sauce and soy sauce and stir to mix. Pour in the stock and add the cornflour paste. Bring to the boil, stirring. Reduce the heat, slide the fish back into the wok and braise gently for about 5 minutes.

Remove the fish. Stir the spring onions, chillies, sugar and sesame oil into the sauce and simmer until reduced. Return the fish to the wok, spoon over the sauce and garnish with fresh coriander.

CHILLI BEAN SAUCE

Commercial chilli bean sauces range from mild to very hot, so add the amount you favour according to the brand used and your taste. You can make your own sauce by mixing dried red chillies, ground in a food processor or pestle and mortar, and yellow bean sauce. A ratio of one part ground chillies to two parts bean sauce will produce a moderately hot result.

Deep-frying and Braising

Because of its gently sloping sides, a wok is an excellent vessel for deep-frying a whole fish in hot oil, and then braising it in a sauce. For safety's sake, use a two-handled wok – it will be more stable than the type with one handle.

Heat the oil in the wok until it is just smoking (about 190°C). Slide in the fish and deep-fry until golden brown on both sides, turning it over with two fish slices.

Braise the fish in the sauce, basting it constantly, until it is cooked through. If the fish is very thick, turn it over with two fish slices halfway through cooking.

FISH STEAK & FILLET PREPARATIONS

Steaks and fillets can be cut from both round and flat fish. The French distinguish between *darnes*, steaks cut from round fish, and *tronçons*, steaks cut from large flat fish. Fish steaks are cut thicker and are quite robust; fish fillets are thinner than steaks and therefore more fragile.

CUTTING ESCALOPES

Large round fish fillets, such as the salmon illustrated here, can be cut into thin slices or escalopes for use in a variety of preparations. Escalopes can be cut from a fillet with or without its skin and should be about 1 cm thick. Often, they are then pounded between sheets of baking parchment to flatten them, making them even thinner. Check for pin bones and remove any you find before you start (see page 12).

Starting near the tail end of the fillet and working your way towards the head, with a sharp, thin-bladed knife, cut evenly sized pieces. Keep the knife almost flat against the fillet as you cut, and always face the tail.

CUTTING STEAKS

Steaks cut from a round fish are made by cutting across one that has been scaled, trimmed and gutted. Use a chef's knife or cleaver. Steaks are usually cut 2.5 cm thick and can be pan-fried, grilled, roasted or poached. Sea bass is shown here.

1 Make evenly spaced marks along the side of the fish. Cut down forcefully through the flesh and backbone at each mark with the knife.

2 Fold the ends of each steak in towards the centre; secure the ends with a wooden cocktail stick to keep the ends from curling during cooking. The steaks are now ready to cook and they can be served with or without the backbone.

MAKING PACKAGES

Thin pieces of fillet called escalopes (see left) can be wrapped around a filling to make a savoury package. Fish packages are fragile and are best poached or carefully pan-fried. Salmon is illustrated here.

1 Put the escalope between two sheets of baking parchment. Pound with a cleaver's flat edge until flat.

2 Wrap the escalope around your chosen filling, making as neat and square a package as possible.

3 Turn the package over seam-side down, and secure it by tying a strip of spring onion around it.

MAKING PILLOWS

A pillow is a piece of fillet in which a pocket is cut to contain a stuffing. Any thick, firm fish, like the salmon shown here, can be used. Cut fillets into 7.5 x 4 cm pieces to accommodate the stuffing. Because they are fragile, pillows are best poached.

1 Starting and ending 1 cm in from each side, cut a pocket in the front of the fillet (do not cut through the back, top or bottom).

2 Hold the pocket open with one hand and spoon the stuffing into the pocket. Do not overfill or the stuffing may burst out during cooking.

3 Secure the opening by tying a strip of spring onion around it. The pillow is now ready for cooking.

MAKING FISH PLAITS

A variety of round and flat fish fillets with contrasting flesh and thin colourful skins, such as the mackerel, snapper and sole shown here, can be used to good effect in this easy but impressive presentation. To preserve the delicate texture of the fillets, steaming is the best cooking method.

1 Cut each fillet into strips about 20 x 2 cm. Lay three strips, one from each fillet, skin-side up on the cutting board. The strips should be close together.

2 Interweave the strips, keeping the plait as even as possible. Plait the strips loosely because they shrink a little when cooked.

3 Steam the plaits (see page 28) over simmering *court bouillon* (see page 24) or fish stock.

MAKING PAUPIETTES

For this technique, skinless fish fillets are halved lengthwise and rolled. They are stuffed before cooking, either by spooning the stuffing on one end of the fish and then rolling it up, or by spooning in the stuffing when the fish rolls are upright. Any flat fish fillet can be used, but the sole shown here, is a classic. Paupiettes are best poached, steamed or baked.

Coil the fillet, skinned-side in, into a turban – the tail end on the outside. To hold the coil, stand them close together during cooking or secure them with wooden cocktail sticks.

FILLINGS FOR FISH PACKAGES, PILLOWS AND PAUPIETTES

Vegetables, fish mousse, soft cheese and herbs are all appropriate. Try one of these:

• A fine julienne of blanched carrots and leeks tossed in vinaigrette.
• Soft cheese and chopped fresh herbs such as parsley or dill.
• Very finely chopped mango, cucumber and fresh root ginger with baby prawns.
• Finely chopped mushrooms and onions sautéed in butter.
• A light, creamy risotto with a hint of lemon.

SMOKED & SALTED FISH

Preserving fish by smoking and salting is traditional. The extra flavour this preparation adds ranges from the subtle to the strong, but preserved fish usually has to be treated further before it is ready to eat.

TARAMASALATA

4 thick slices of white bread, crusts removed

6 tbsp milk

100 g prepared smoked cod's roe (see right)

2 garlic cloves, chopped

100 ml olive oil

100 ml vegetable oil

About 75 ml lemon juice

2 tbsp hot water

Freshly ground pepper

Tear the bread into a bowl and add the milk. Mix well with your hands, then squeeze the bread and discard the milk. Put the bread in a food processor and blend with the smoked cod's roe, garlic, olive oil, groundnut oil and 75 ml lemon juice. Add the water, then taste and add pepper, and more lemon juice if you like. Blend again until mixed.

Turn out the mixture into a bowl, cover and let chill in the refrigerator for at least 4 hours, preferably overnight. Serves 4–6.

PREPARING SMOKED ROE

The roe, or eggs, of the female salmon, trout or cod (as shown here) is often sold salted and smoked. Once soaked, it can be eaten raw, thinly sliced and sprinkled with lemon juice and ground pepper. It can also be used in creamy dips such as Greek taramasalata (see box, left).

Cut the smoked cod's roe into pieces, place in a bowl and pour over enough boiling water to cover. Soak for 1–2 minutes, then drain thoroughly. Peel away the skin with your fingers and discard. The flesh is now ready to use.

DESALTING ANCHOVIES

Anchovies are sold in cans or jars, salted and packed in oil. The best of the preserved anchovies are the fillets that come from the Mediterranean, available here in continental delicatessens. They are bottled in olive oil and are not too salty. Canned anchovies contain more salt and will therefore need to be desalted. This technique will make them slightly softer in texture and milder in flavour.

1 Turn the anchovies into a sieve set over a bowl and let the oil drain through. Discard the oil. Turn the anchovies into the bowl.

2 Pour in enough cold milk to cover the anchovies and let soak for 20 minutes. Drain off the milk, rinse the anchovies under cold running water and pat dry.

PREPARING SALT COD

Salt cod is very popular in Portugal, where it is called bacalhau, and in Spain, where it is known as bacalao. The whole gutted fish or fillets are soaked in brine or layered with dry salt, then dried. It is available from ethnic shops and delicatessens. Before cooking it must be soaked to reconstitute it and remove the excess salt.

Cut the fish into pieces, place in a bowl and cover with cold water. Let soak for at least 2 days for heavily salted fish, changing the water 5–6 times. After soaking, drain the fish, then place in a pan of cold water and bring to just below boiling point. Simmer for 20 minutes or until tender. Flake into meaty chunks, discarding all skin and bones.

USING SLICED SMOKED SALMON

Line ramekins with salmon, fill with *taramasalata* (see opposite page) and turn out.

SLICING SMOKED SALMON

For a large party it is more economical to buy a whole side of salmon and slice it yourself than to buy it ready sliced. A smoked salmon knife (see box, right) makes light work of this technique, although any long, thin flexible knife can be used.

Trim and discard the dark fatty edges and remove any pin bones (see page 12). Holding the knife as parallel to the fish as possible and starting at the tail end, cut wafer thin slices with a gentle sawing action. Work along the fish towards the head end, cutting slices in "V" shapes so the dark fatty flesh in the centre is not included. For easy serving, interleave the slices with non-stick paper.

SMOKED SALMON KNIFE

To slice smoked salmon very thinly you can buy a special smoked salmon slicer. This is a knife with a long, narrow, flexible blade. The cutting edge is straight but the blade can be smooth or fluted and is usually rounded at the tip. Its smoothness and flexibility enables it to slice through the soft salmon flesh without tearing it. The knife can also be used to slice *gravadlax* very thinly on the diagonal (see below).

MAKING GRAVADLAX

In Sweden, they have perfected the art of salting fish to produce the famous gravadlax. *Use unskinned salmon fillets; once cured, store wrapped in the refrigerator for up to 2 days.*

1 Lay two 900 g salmon fillets skin-side down in a shallow glass dish. Combine 75 g sea salt, 125 g sugar and 2 tsp crushed white peppercorns and sprinkle over the fish. Sprinkle 1 large bunch of coarsely chopped dill evenly over the salt mixture.

2 Lay the uncoated fillet, skin-side up over the other. Place foil-covered cardboard over the fillets and weight it down. Refrigerate for 3 days, turning every 12 hours until the seasonings have penetrated the flesh.

3 To serve, separate the two fillets and cut each one crosswise on the diagonal into thin slices. Fan the slices out on individual plates and serve with lemon and dill, and a mustard and dill sauce.

Sushi & Sashimi

These well-known Japanese dishes are much enjoyed in the West.
Sushi is based on vinegared rice rolled in seaweed, with strips of raw fish or
a vegetable such as cucumber or avocado hidden in the centre. Sashimi is
simply very fresh raw fish, served with a horseradish paste called wasabi.
Both are exquisitely presented, and are eaten with chopsticks.

Sushi Rolls

MAKES 32 SLICES

1 piece of very fresh tuna fillet, about 200 g, skinned

4 sheets of nori seaweed, each measuring 20 x 18 cm

Rice vinegar

600 g vinegared rice

Wasabi (see box, right)

TO SERVE

Pickled ginger roses (see page 27)

Cucumber crowns

Japanese soy sauce

Cut the tuna crosswise into strips, each 1 cm wide.

If the nori is not labelled *"yakinori"* – pre-toasted – hold each sheet with tongs and wave one side over a gas flame for a few seconds until crisp.

Place a rolling mat flat on the work surface and put a sheet of nori on top, close to one of the short edges of the mat. Dip your fingers in water mixed with a dash of rice vinegar, and spread a layer of vinegared rice over the nori. Make a line of wasabi paste in the centre of the rice and cover with tuna.

Roll the nori around the rice with the mat. Press the mat around the roll to keep the shape tight. Run a wet fingertip along the exposed edge of the nori to seal it. Using a moistened chef's knife, cut the roll across into eight pieces. Repeat four times.

Arrange the sushi rolls, cut side-up, on a platter. Serve with ginger roses, cucumber crowns and soy sauce.

Sashimi

SERVES 4

1 piece of very fresh red mullet fillet, about 200 g, scaled but not skinned

1 piece of very fresh salmon fillet, about 400 g, skinned

About 300 g very fresh mackerel fillet, unskinned, with membrane removed

TO SERVE

Cucumber crowns
Wasabi (see box, right)
Japanese soy sauce

Before cutting the fish, check that all bones, especially fine pin bones, have been removed. The fish will be much easier to cut thinly if it is very well chilled.

Cut the piece of red mullet fillet into very thin slices against the grain.

Cut the mackerel fillets lengthwise in half. Holding the halves together, skin-side up, cut the fish across into thin slices, the same thickness as the red mullet and salmon.

Arrange the mullet, salmon and mackerel slices on plates, keeping them separate. Serve with cucumber crowns, wasabi and soy sauce.

WASABI

Known as Japanese horseradish because of its hot, pungent flavour, wasabi comes from the root of an Oriental plant. It is used freshly grated in Japan, but in the West it is normally sold as a paste, ready prepared in tubes. Look for it in large supermarkets.

Making Sushi Rolls

Individual sushi rolls are cut from one long roll to reveal the filling hidden in the centre.
For shaping the long roll you need to use a mat. Special bamboo rolling mats can be found in Oriental shops, or you can use an undyed, flexible straw place mat.

Lay tuna over the line of wasabi paste to cover it completely. You may need more than one strip of tuna.

Lift up the short end of the mat nearest to you and roll the nori around the rice, rolling it away from you.

Cut the long sushi roll across into four equal lengths, then cut each length in half to make eight pieces.

POACHING FISH

Fish is often cooked in liquid kept just below boiling point because this gentle method of cooking helps preserve the delicate nature of the flesh. Large whole fish are traditionally poached in a *court bouillon*.

COURT BOUILLON

2.5 litres water
700 ml dry white wine
250 ml white wine vinegar
2 carrots, chopped
2 onions, chopped
1 large bouquet garni
1¹/₂ tsp rock or sea salt
2 tsp black peppercorns

Combine all ingredients, except vinegar, in a large pan. Bring to the boil, then simmer, uncovered, for 15–20 minutes, adding the vinegar for the last 5 minutes. Cool before use. Store in the refrigerator for up to 5 days. Makes about 3 litres.

MICROWAVE TIMES

Delicate fish flesh requires quick cooking. The speed of the microwave ensures that the flesh remains moist and cooks evenly. The cooking times shown below are for 600–700 watt ovens set to 100% power.

• STEAKS
   2–3 mins per 250 g

• FILLETS
   45 secs–1 min per 175 g

• PACKAGES AND PAUPIETTES
   1¹/₂–2 mins each
   with precooked filling

• WHOLE FLAT FISH
   1¹/₂–2 mins per 250 g

• WHOLE ROUND FISH
   2¹/₂–3 mins per 250 g unstuffed

POACHING IN A KETTLE

Whole fish with the head on, or off such as the salmon used here, must be trimmed, scaled and gutted before cooking. Stovetop poaching affords you most control. A fish kettle is made for this task – the entire fish fits comfortably on a rack in the cooking vessel, with enough room for the poaching liquid to cover it.

1 Measure the thickest part of the fish. Put the fish on the rack and lower into the kettle. Cover the fish with cold *court bouillon*. Check seasoning. Bring to the boil.

2 Reduce to a simmer. Poach the fish for 10 minutes for each 2.5 cm width. Cool the fish in the kettle to retain moisture. Remove and turn out on to baking parchment (see page 25).

POACHING WITHOUT A KETTLE

Fish kettles are convenient for cooking a large whole fish, such as a salmon or sea bass, but if you don't want to go to the expense of buying a piece of equipment that may be used only rarely, you can improvize with everyday equipment.

Cut and fold a double or triple thickness of foil slightly larger than the fish. Lay the fish on one of its sides on the foil and place in a large roasting tin. Pour cold *court bouillon* (see box, above left) over the fish to just cover it, then cover the pan with foil and cook and cool as in the fish kettle (see above). Lift out the fish with the aid of the foil. The fish can now be prepared for serving (see page 25).

SHALLOW POACHING

This technique suits steaks, fillets, and small whole fish that are scaled and gutted.

Lower the fish into a pan of simmering *court bouillon*. Bring back to a simmer and cover. Poach, allowing 5–10 minutes for fillets and 10–15 minutes for steaks, until opaque throughout.

POACHING SMOKED FISH

Smoked fish, such as haddock and cod, is usually poached in seasoned milk rather than court bouillon *or* water. *Milk helps rid the fish of excess salt and mellows its smoky flavour.*

1 Pour milk or an equal mixture of milk and water into a pan and add 1–2 bay leaves and a few peppercorns. Add the smoked fish, bring to a simmer over a moderate heat, then remove from the heat and cover tightly. Let stand for 10 minutes. Remove the fish and discard milk and flavourings.

2 Scrape away the skin and any dark flesh with a paring knife. Turn the fish over and remove any bones with tweezers.

USING POACHED SMOKED FISH

Even a small amount of smoked fish will add a unique flavour to many dishes. After poaching flake the flesh and use it as follows:

• Mix with curried rice and chopped hard-boiled eggs to make a kedgeree.
• Use to flavour a hot soufflé.
• Toss with salad leaves and serve with horseradish cream.

PREPARING A WHOLE POACHED FISH FOR SERVING

For easy serving and eating, remove the skin and bones of a whole poached fish, such as the salmon shown here. If you follow the method below, the fish can still be presented whole so it will look attractive, an important consideration if you are serving the fish as a table centrepiece. The fish can be served hot or cold.

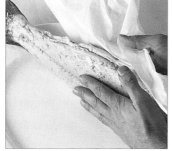

3 Repeating steps 1 and 2, peel away the skin and scrape the dark flesh from the reverse side. Carefully split the top fillet of the fish using a chef's knife, then lay the pieces to either side.

1 After poaching (see page 24) turn the fish on to baking parchment. Cut along the backbone. Working from head to tail, peel away skin.

2 Scrape away any dark flesh with a chef's knife. Roll the fish from the paper on to a serving plate.

4 Lift out the backbone, bringing the rib bones out with it, if necessary, cutting it from the tail end of the fish with kitchen scissors.

5 Put both of the top fillets back in place. The fish is now ready to coat with a sauce or garnish (see pages 26–27).

FINISHING TOUCHES

Lemon slices and fresh parsley are classic garnishes for fish dishes and the latter is useful to hide an open eye. Other fruit, vegetable and herb decorations, however, will add interest and colour to the presentation. Rose petal scales secured in aspic (see opposite page) are the most fanciful.

PRESENTING A WHOLE FISH

Small fish are normally served whole, skin and bones in place, larger fish are more often skinned and filleted, then reformed and presented whole. This is usually the case with poached salmon (see page 25), which is classically garnished with overlapping cucumber "scales". For a colourful and summery presentation, use fresh rose petals instead of cucumber (see opposite page), dipping their tips in aspic or mayonnaise so they will adhere to the fish. Courgette scales are another option.

KEEP IT SIMPLE

• Serve lemon wedges for squeezing fresh juice over fish. For formal occasions, wrap the wedges in muslin so the seeds do not scatter on the fish.
• Use dainty bunches or sprigs of fresh herbs, such as those on the opposite page. Chervil, chives, lemon balm and watercress are other options.
• Add finely chopped herbs or watercress to mayonnaise and serve with poached fish, especially salmon.
• Serve hot fish topped with pats of chilled maître d'hôtel (parsley and lemon) butter. Anchovy and citrus butters are also good with fish.

ZESTY KNOTS
Use a canelle knife to cut 4-cm strips of lime, lemon or orange zest. Blanch, then dry and knot.

CAPER FLOWERS
With your fingertips, gently pull back some of the outer layers of drained capers to make petals.

ANCHOVY LOOPS
Drain canned anchovy fillets and pat dry, then cut into strips. Wrap anchovy strips around capers.

KUMQUAT CUPS
Make small angled cuts all round a kumquat's middle, then pull apart. Top with mayonnaise and fresh dill.

LIME BUTTERFLIES
Cut lime slices into quarters, then join 2 points to make a bow. Top with a star cut from a blanched red pepper strip.

PASTRY FLEURONS
Cut shapes from rolled-out puff pastry. Brush with an egg-yolk glaze; bake at 190°C until golden, 5–7 minutes.

LEMON SPECIAL
Cut top and bottom off lemon. Cut strips of zest, leaving them attached at top. Weave strips as shown.

CITRUS CURLS
Cut a 15-cm strip of orange peel with a canelle knife. Curl around a skewer until the peel holds the shape.

WINGED LEMON
Canelle a lemon. Cut around 180° leaving one end attached; rotate lemon and repeat. Fold one cut point over another.

ASIAN DECORATIONS

Chinese and Japanese steamed whole fish and stir-fried dishes benefit from traditional decorations made from ingredients sold in Asian food stores and large supermarkets. Buy sliced, not shredded pickled ginger.

DEEP-FRIED GINGER
Blanch julienned peeled fresh root ginger; pat dry. Deep-fry in 180°C oil for 10 seconds, then drain.

MOOLI JULIENNE
Cut a peeled mooli crosswise into thin slices, then into julienne strips. Keep crisp in iced water, then pat dry.

PICKLED GINGER ROSE
Roll up one slice to form the centre, then wrap 3 more overlapping slices around the first to form "petals".

SPRING ONION TASSEL
Slice the green end of a spring onion lengthwise, leaving one end uncut. Chill in water for 2–3 hours until curled.

DEEP-FRIED HERBS
Deep-fry leafy herbs, such as purple basil and flat-leaf parsley, in 180°C oil for 10 seconds. Drain well.

CUCUMBER TWIRLS
Rib a cucumber with a canelle knife and cut into wafer-thin slices. Slit each slice and twist.

HERB BOUQUET
Fan out sprigs of fresh parsley, dill or thyme next to freshly cooked fish. Tarragon is also suitable.

LEMON ZEST ROSE
Use a very sharp knife to pare a long strip of zest in a spiral, giving it a "frilly" edge. Roll up to make a rose blossom.

COURGETTE SCALES
Blanch a courgette, cut into slices, then quarters. Lay quarters over fish so they overlap like scales.

STEAMING FISH

The vapour produced by a simmering liquid cooks fish by steaming. This method is ideal for delicate fish, such as sole and plaice, and shellfish. Water can be used, but a vegetable or herb broth adds flavour.

FLAVOURING THE FISH

Steamed fish can be bland so give flavour to it by adding vegetables, herbs and spices, and other seasonings to the liquid in the wok or steamer, or by sprinkling them over the fish itself.

- Chop a mixture of herbs and vegetables – onions, carrots, celery, fennel, parsley stalks or coriander leaves – and add to the steaming liquid.
- Place the fish on the steaming rack on a thick bed of fresh fennel fronds and fresh sprigs of thyme or dill.
- Cover the fish with chopped spring onions, slivers of fresh root ginger or garlic and slices of lemon and a sprinkling of fennel seeds.
- Marinate the fish before steaming. Olive oil, lemon juice, white wine and soy sauce are are all good with fish.

STEAMING TIMES

Fish is cooked when opaque throughout and the flakes separate easily with a fork. If overcooked, the fish will be dry and fall apart.

- FILLETS
  3–4 mins

- PLAITS
  8–10 mins

- WHOLE FISH
  6–8 mins (up to 350 g)
  12–15 mins (up to 900 g)

CONVENTIONAL METHOD

Metal steamers contain perforated baskets that sit above the simmering liquid at the bottom. Steam filters through the perforations and cooks the fish. Here, plaits of mackerel, snapper and sole (see page 19) are steamed over a simmering court bouillon.

1 Add *court bouillon* to cover the bottom of the steamer and bring to a simmer. Arrange the fish in a single layer in the basket. Place the basket over the simmering liquid. Cover and steam (see chart, below left).

2 The fish is ready when it is opaque. Test it with a fork: the flesh should feel moist and tender.

BAMBOO STEAMER METHOD

A woven basket can be placed in a wok over simmering broth. The aromatic steam helps flavour the fish, while herbs, spices and other seasonings can be added to the fish itself. Steaming preserves the attractive colour of fish, such as the red snapper shown here.

2 Score the fish and insert flavourings of your choice (see page 11) so the flavours enter the flesh. Lay the fish flat in the basket and sprinkle over more flavourings. Place the basket in the wok.

1 Half fill a wok with water and bring to a simmer. Add chopped vegetables (see box, above left).

3 Place the lid on the basket to intensify the flavour imparted by the vegetables and other additions. Steam according to the times given in the chart, left. Serve with the steamed vegetables and seasonings.

GRILLING FISH

The high heat of the grill and barbecue cooks fish quickly which is by far the best way. Fatty fish such as sardines and mackerel are ideal, their natural oils help keep the flesh moist during cooking.

GRILLING SMALL WHOLE FISH

Skin and bones keep fish moist so it is best to grill fish whole. Trim, scale and gut the fish (see pages 10–11) before cooking and score (see page 11) if you like. For additional flavour, marinate in olive oil, crushed garlic and chopped parsley as shown here with the sardines.

1 Remove the fish from the marinade and place on an oiled grill rack. Grill under a high heat for 2 minutes.

2 Turn the fish over and brush with the marinade, or with olive oil if a marinade was not used. Grill for another 2 minutes, or until the skin is crisp and golden.

BARBECUING WHOLE FISH

The heat of the barbecue sears the fish keeping the flesh moist and flavourful. Trout is shown here but other suitable fish include mackerel, shark, tuna and bass. For even cooking, score the fish (see page 11), and for ease of handling, use a fish rack (see box, above right).

Place the fish in an oiled rack, with sprigs of fresh herbs or vine leaves if you like, and close the rack tightly. Place the rack on the grid of a hot barbecue. Cook the fish for about 3 minutes on each side, basting frequently with olive oil or marinade. Check for doneness: the skin should be crisp and golden and the flesh fork-tender.

FISH RACKS

Whether barbecuing whole fish, fillets or steaks, a special hinged fish rack can make the job more manageable. Brush the fish rack with olive oil to prevent the fish from sticking to it.

FISH-SHAPED RACK

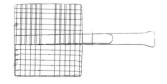

SQUARE RACK

SALSA FOR FISH

Contrast a cooked fish straight from the barbecue with a chilled spicy salsa.

A traditional accompaniment in Mexican cooking, *salsa* combines pungent garlic, onion and chillies with the sharp tang of lime. Served chilled *salsa* brings out the subtle flavours of hot fish.

BAKING FISH

This is an excellent method for cooking large and medium-sized whole fish and for thick steaks and fillets. Fish can be baked without a covering, or wrapped in parcels of foil, paper or leaves or, for a whole fish, baked with a salt crust. For a more substantial dish, fish can be stuffed before baking; this will also give the fish more flavour.

FLAVOURINGS FOR OPEN BAKING

The simplest flavouring is fresh herbs pushed into the stomach cavity. Some alternatives are:

- Asian flavourings such as fresh ginger and lemon grass.
- Fresh breadcrumbs with herbs, spices or chopped nuts bound with egg.
- Prawns with garlic or parsley.

OPEN BAKING

Medium-sized whole fish such as red snapper are ideal for cooking this way.

Place a single layer of fish in a greased roasting tin. Sprinkle over flavourings (see box, left) and just cover with liquid. Bake, uncovered, at 180°C for 30 minutes or until the flesh is opaque and the skin crisp. If you like, strain the pan juices and serve with the fish.

STUFFING AND BAKING IN FOIL

A foil wrapping allows fish to cook in its own juices, keeping it deliciously moist. The fish can be wrapped unstuffed or, depending on the boning method can be stuffed through the stomach or back. Stuffed fish take a little longer to cook.

1 Spoon your chosen stuffing into the stomach cavity of the fish. Secure the stomach opening with 1–2 wooden cocktail sticks.

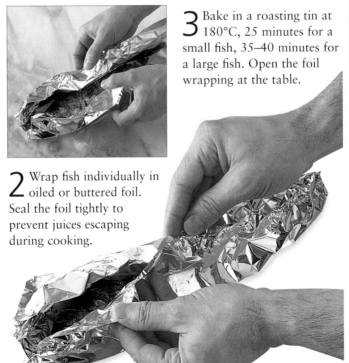

2 Wrap fish individually in oiled or buttered foil. Seal the foil tightly to prevent juices escaping during cooking.

3 Bake in a roasting tin at 180°C, 25 minutes for a small fish, 35–40 minutes for a large fish. Open the foil wrapping at the table.

STUFFING THROUGH THE BACK BEFORE BAKING

Though the back cavity is smaller than the stomach, stuffing the back enables the fish to maintain a good shape. For the technique of boning a whole fish through the back, see page 13.

Spoon the stuffing into the cavity in the back of the fish. Wrap and bake as for the fish shown left.

BAKING EN PAPILLOTE

The term en papillote *is French for "in a paper bag". This technique protects the fish (brill is shown here) and helps keep it moist. The topping of herbs, vegetables and white wine adds flavour during cooking. For maximum effect, open the parcels at the table.*

1 Cut a heart shape, 5 cm larger than the fish, out of baking parchment, grease-proof paper or foil, and oil it.

2 Put the fish on one half with 4 sprigs of coriander, 2 carrots, julienned, and 4 tbsp white wine.

3 Fold over the other half of the paper and twist to seal the edges. Place on a baking sheet and bake at 180°C for 15–20 minutes, until puffed.

BAKING IN LEAVES

Vine and banana leaves keep fish moist during cooking and they also flavour the fish.

Set the fish in the centre of a leaf. Roll and wrap the leaf around the fish. Tie in place with a blanched strip of leek if necessary.

BAKING IN A SALT CRUST

Fish baked in this way will have a crispy skin and moist flesh – without being over salty. The salt crust will help the fish to retain moisture and add flavour. Before cooking, trim, scale and gut, then wipe the fish dry with paper towels.

1 Spread a 5 cm layer of sea salt evenly over the bottom of a heavy-based casserole dish. Lay the fish on top of the salt and cover with another salt layer (1.3 kg salt will cover 900 g fish as shown here).

2 Sprinkle the salt with water. Bake the fish at 220°C for about 30 minutes.

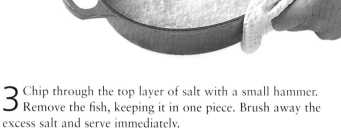

3 Chip through the top layer of salt with a small hammer. Remove the fish, keeping it in one piece. Brush away the excess salt and serve immediately.

TRICK OF THE TRADE

PLAITED MONKFISH

Plait rindless streaky bacon rashers around a monkfish fillet, tucking in a few thyme leaves as you go. Bake at 180°C for 20 minutes. During baking the bacon imparts flavour to the fish and forms a crunchy coating; the fat seeps into the fish to moisten it.

FRYING FISH

Choose pieces of fish of equal thickness to ensure even cooking. The temperature of the fat, whether oil or butter, is vital – too low and the coating will be soggy and fall apart, too high and it will cook too quickly.

COATINGS FOR FISH

A light coating protects delicate fish fillets and helps keep them moist during frying.

- Make a dry blend of Cajun herbs and spices – paprika, onion and garlic powder, dried thyme and oregano, white, black and cayenne pepper and salt.
- Mix fragrant herbs and spices such as chopped fresh dill, crushed fennel seeds and coarsely ground pepper.
- Mix snipped chives and a little grated lemon zest into fine breadcrumbs or flour.

SHALLOW PAN-FRYING

Use equal parts butter and vegetable oil for successful pan-frying. Season and coat the fish first (see box, left) and ensure the butter is foaming before adding fish.

1 Place the fish, skin-side down, in foaming butter and oil. Fry for 5 minutes then turn the fish over.

2 Fry the fillets for another 3–5 minutes, until golden brown. Insert a fork into the thickest part of the flesh – it should feel firm and be opaque throughout.

NUT-BROWN BUTTER

Called beurre noisette *in French, this is the classic butter for frying white fish, especially skate wings. Remove the dark skin and coat with seasoned flour.*

Heat 4 tbsp butter in a frying pan until it turns a light nutty brown. Add the skate wings and fry for 8–10 minutes, turning once.

CAJUN-STYLE

Fish fried Cajun-style, from New Orleans and the states around the Gulf of Mexico, has a dark, peppery-hot crust. This comes from the special coating that is generously rubbed over it before cooking (see box, above left).

Place coated fish fillets (red snapper is shown here) in hot fat. Fry until the coating is charred, about 6 minutes, turning once.

COATING WITH A HERB CRUST

This technique creates an attractive crust, which adds contrast in flavour and texture to the moist fish. Use firm textured fillets such as salmon, cod or monkfish. A non-stick pan reduces the oil required, allowing the crust to "toast".

1 Spread a mixture of fragrant herbs and spices (see box, above left) over a plate. Press skinned fish fillets, skinned-side down, into the mixture to ensure an even coating.

2 Pan-fry the fillets, crust-side down, in a little hot oil for 7–10 minutes without turning. Press firmly with a metal spatula to encourage the juices to rise to the surface and the heat to penetrate upwards into the flesh.

DEEP-FRYING FISH IN BATTER

Batter provides a protective coating, which keeps fish succulent and moist. A high cooking temperature (180–190°C) is necessary for the best result, and the oil should be carefully chosen, both for its ability to reach the required temperature and how it affects the flavour of the fish; vegetable oils are best. Cut the fish into even pieces or use steaks or fillets.

1 To test the temperature of the oil, drop in a cube of white bread, it should brown all over in about 30 seconds. Remove the bread and discard.

2 Lower the batter-coated fish into the hot oil. Cook large pieces of fish one at a time for 7–10 minutes to ensure even cooking.

3 When golden and crisp, lift the basket out of the fryer. Shake the basket to remove excess oil, then drain the fish on to paper towels. Season before serving.

MAKING GOUJONS

Cut strips from skinned fish fillets, working across the grain of the flesh: this helps the goujons retain their shape. The oil will rise in the pan, so fill to the recommended level – a deep pan should be filled to one-third of its capacity.

1 Cut the skinned fish fillets into 1-cm strips, working across the grain and using a chef's knife.

2 Put the strips of fish in a plastic bag containing seasoned flour. Twist the top to seal, and shake to coat evenly.

3 Heat the oil to 180–190°C. Lower the goujons into the oil using a slotted spoon or fryer basket. Deep fry for 3–4 minutes until golden. Remove and drain on paper towels.

FISH MIXTURES

Many fish can be puréed or flaked and the resulting mixtures have many applications. Fish mousse can be moulded, layered or shaped into dumplings, and flaked fish can be formed into cakes. Enliven the basic fish mousse shown here with chopped herbs, ground spices or other seasonings.

FISH MOUSSE

450 g fish fillets (whiting, plaice,
   sole or salmon)
Salt
2 egg whites
350 ml whipping or double cream
Ground white pepper or cayenne

Trim and skin the fish fillets and remove all of the bones, checking carefully for any pin bones. Purée the flesh in a food processor with salt to taste, then add the egg whites. For a velvety texture, pass this mixture through a fine sieve into a bowl (this will also help eliminate any fine pin bones that may remain). Gradually fold in the cream over an ice bath to prevent the mixture from splitting. Season with salt and pepper. Makes about 850 g.

WHAT'S IN A NAME?

QUENELLES: The word derives from the German word for dumpling, *knödel*, but it now means any egg-shaped sweet or savoury mixture such as mousse and sorbet. Small quenelles can be used to garnish clear soups.
TIMBALES: This is the name given to small, round, deep moulds and also to any food that is shaped or baked in them, as long as it forms a single serving. The name can be applied to fish, meat or vegetable preparations.

MAKING A FISH MOUSSE

Chilling the mixture over an ice bath when adding the cream prevents the mixture from separating.

1 Chop the fish into chunks and purée evenly with the salt in a food processor fitted with the metal blade. Add the egg whites and process until evenly incorporated.

2 Work the mixture through a sieve into a bowl, then set it over a bowl of water and ice cubes. Fold in the cream with a rubber spatula.

MAKING FISH TIMBALES

One of the simplest ways to use the fish mousse above is to bake it in dariole moulds.

1 Divide the mousse between 6 chilled dariole moulds. Cover with buttered grease-proof paper. Set in a roasting tin and pour in hot water almost to the top of moulds.

2 Bake in a *bain marie* at 160° C until firm, about 25 minutes. Turn out on to individual plates.

MAKING FISH QUENELLES

These dumplings, made from the fish mousse above, are shaped with tablespoons that have been dipped in water.

1 Take one spoonful of mousse and round each side with another spoon until smooth and egg-shaped. Repeat to make 18 quenelles.

2 Poach the quenelles until firm, 5–10 minutes. Remove with a slotted spoon, and drain on paper towels.

MAKING FISH CAKES

These can be made from a variety of different raw fish: white fish such as cod or hake, or oily fish such as mackerel or salmon. A mixture of fresh and smoked fish is also good, and the fish can be coarsely flaked or finely minced, whichever you prefer.

Leftover cooked fish can also be used in fish cakes, using equal quantities of fish and potatoes.

1 Flake raw fish with a fork. Mix with mashed potato and enough egg to bind, using a spatula. Add chopped parsley and seasonings and blend into the mixture.

2 Form the mixture into balls, flatten them and coat in dried breadcrumbs. Let chill for 30 minutes. Pan-fry in hot oil for 5–6 minutes on each side or until golden.

MAKING A LAYERED FISH TERRINE

Here the basic fish mousse (see box, opposite page) is given an elegant treatment in a terrine with three layers. One layer uses the basic mixture, another uses the basic mixture with liquefied herbs, and spinach-wrapped prawns are sandwiched in between. If you like, add contrast by making half the mousse with salmon or trout. The terrine can be served hot or cold.

1 Line a buttered terrine mould with blanched spinach leaves, making sure that there are no gaps.

2 Roll up the prawns in blanched spinach leaves and place on top of the plain mousse in three rows.

3 Cover the spinach-wrapped prawns with the fish mousse to which liquefied herbs have been added. Pipe it in even rows so that the finished texture will be smooth. Once baked, turn out and serve sliced. If serving the terrine cold, as shown here, serve slices on a saffron sauce garnished with saffron strands.

FISH TERRINE

*850 g fish mousse
  (see opposite page)
300 g cooked peeled prawns
12–15 large spinach leaves,
  blanched
30 g mixed chervil and dill,
  chopped*

Liquefy the chopped chervil and dill in a food processor. Divide the mousse in half and add the liquefied herbs to one half until the mousse is a rich green colour.

Line a buttered 1.5 litre terrine with blanched spinach. Pipe a layer of the plain fish mousse in the terrine. Wrap the prawns in blanched spinach, arrange on the plain mousse and pipe a layer of the herb mousse on top. Cover with baking parchment. Bake in a *bain marie* at 150°C for about 1 hour or until a knife inserted in the centre comes out clean. Turn out and serve sliced, hot or cold.

LOBSTER

A lobster's flesh is meaty, sweet and delicate. For absolute freshness, lobsters are best bought live and prepared at home. Choose active ones that feel heavy for their size.

HUMANE KILLING

Some chefs recommend placing the live lobster in the freezer for an hour to desensitize it before killing.

Hold the lobster, back up and claws bound, firmly on a cutting board. Locate the centre of the cross-shaped mark on the back and pierce through to the board with the point of a chef's knife. This kills instantly, but there may be some twitching from the severed nerves. You can now cut the lobster as required.

WHAT'S IN A NAME?

The term *en bellevue* is used to describe cold dishes of shellfish, fish and poultry glazed in aspic jelly, giving them a smooth, attractive finish. For lobster, the meat is sliced, glazed and arranged in the shell.

It seems that the name came from the Château de Belleville, owned in the 1750s by Madame Pompadour, who stimulated the appetite of Louis XV with attractively presented dishes.

COOKING A LIVE LOBSTER

Lobsters are usually bought with rubber bands tied around the claws and the tail braced with string tied to a piece of wood.

1 Leaving the body support intact, plunge the lobster into a deep pan of boiling *court bouillon* (see page 66).

2 Bring back to the boil and cook until the shell turns red, 5 minutes per initial 450 g, plus 3 minutes for each extra 450 g. Transfer the cooked lobster with a slotted spoon to a colander. Drain and let cool.

REMOVING THE TAIL MEAT FROM ITS SHELL

Cooked lobster can be served in numerous ways. The tail meat, one of the most succulent parts, is generally removed in one piece and sliced into neat pieces known as medallions.

1 Remove body support. With the lobster belly-side up, cut through the shell along each side of the tail.

2 Pull the shell back, exposing the meat of the lobster tail.

3 Pull tail meat from shell, keeping it whole. Make a shallow cut along the inner curve. Remove dark vein.

4 Cut away the white flesh from the top of the tail meat, then cut the remaining flesh into even slices. Present them overlapping along the back of the lobster – when glazed with aspic this presentation is called *en bellevue* (see box, left).

REMOVING MEAT FROM THE HALF-SHELL

The orangey-red shell of a cooked lobster makes an attractive serving "dish". The entire tail section can be detached from the head, rinsed out and used for serving. Alternatively, and especially when the lobster is intended for two, you can serve the meat on the half-shell.

2 Spoon out the green liver, or tomalley, and reserve. Female lobsters may contain roe, or coral, which is pink when cooked and should be saved. Discard the gravel sac.

1 Cook the lobster as described on the opposite page. When it is cool enough to handle comfortably, cut the string and remove the body support. Holding the lobster with its back uppermost, and cut it in half lengthwise from head to tail with a large chef's knife.

3 Gently pull the tail meat from each side of the shell. Remove and discard the intestinal vein.

4 Crack each claw just below the pincer, without damaging the meat. Remove meat from base of claw shell.

5 Pull the small pincer away from the rest of the claw, bringing with it the flat white membrane. Remove the meat from this part of the claw. Pull the meat from the large pincer shell, keeping it in one piece.

LOBSTER CRACKERS

Lobster claws are especially tough. To remove their meat, use a cracking tool or small hammer.

Lobster crackers are similar to the hinged type of nut crackers but are rather sturdier. The inner edges near the hinge are ridged to provide grip on the smooth shells. Some have a prong at the end to tease out the claw meat. You can also buy lobster pincers designed to crack the claws and extract the meat.

PARTS OF A LOBSTER

The lobster's shell accounts for two-thirds of its weight, but very little of the rest is inedible. Blue-black when raw, the shell turns scarlet when cooked.

CLAW   GRAVEL SAC   ROE

GILLS   TOMALLEY   TAIL MEAT

EDIBLE PARTS
- The most meaty part is the lobster tail.
- The two claws are also full of delicious flesh.
- The green, creamy liver (tomalley) is a delicacy.
- In the female, the roe can be eaten. It is black when raw and scarlet when cooked.

INEDIBLE PARTS
- The shell and legs.
- The bony membranes in the two claws.
- Small gravel sac (the stomach).
- The intestinal channel which runs down the back to the tail.
- The feathery gills in the body section between the lobster's head and tail.

37

CRAB

There are over twelve edible varieties of crab, the large-bodied species being the most common in the kitchen. You can buy crab whole, alive or cooked – live ones should be active and feel heavy for their size. Crabs are usually cooked whole and then cut up afterwards.

BOILING A CRAB

The cooking liquid can vary from water or the classic court bouillon (see page 24) to a spicy broth (see box, left). Before you start, put the live crab in the freezer for 1 hour to desensitize it. The crab will then be easy to handle.

1 If not already done by the fishmonger, tie the crab with string to keep its claws still. Fill a pan with enough *court bouillon* to cover the crab. Bring to the boil.

2 Add the crab and cover the pan; bring back to the boil and cook until the shell of the crab turns red, about 5 minutes per 450 g.

3 Remove the cooked crab from the pan with a slotted spoon. Transfer to a colander to drain. Let cool, then remove the cooked meat from the shell (see below).

HOW TO DRESS CRAB

This classic presentation turns the large shell into an elegant container for the crab. Remove meat, keeping pieces as large as possible. Pick over crab and remove any membrane or shell. Cut around the line rimming the edge of shell. Scrub out shell and dry. Arrange white meat in one half of shell. Mix any brown meat with a little mayonnaise and pile into the other half. Garnish with finely chopped fresh parsley, finely chopped hard-boiled egg white and sieved hard-boiled egg yolk; serve with additional mayonnaise.

REMOVING COOKED CRABMEAT FROM THE SHELL

Although size and shape vary from one species to another, the essential parts of the body need a similar approach. The larger the crab the easier it is to remove the meat. A variety of utensils are available to extract the meat. For the legs, snip open the shell and remove the meat with a pick. Use a spoon to scoop out the yellowish-brown meat from the shell. Opt for a skewer or larding needle to poke out the white fibres from the central body. To dress a crab, see box (left).

1 Hold the legs and claws close to the body and twist to remove. Discard the legs.

2 Crack the claws without damaging the meat inside. Remove the meat in large chunks.

3 Remove the pointed tail or apron flap by snapping it back with your fingers.

4 Break the shell by pressing down each side of the body with your thumbs. Lift out the body section. Scrape away the soft brown meat from the shell, keeping it separate from the white claw meat.

5 Discard the stomach sac and soft gills (also known as dead man's fingers) as they are inedible. If you intend to use the shell for serving, clean it thoroughly.

6 Cut the body of the crab in half lengthwise with a chef's knife. Remove the meat from the body of the crab with the handle of a small spoon or a chopstick, keeping it separate from the brown shell meat.

PRAWNS

The different varieties and sizes of prawns available are enormous, but no matter what sort you buy, the techniques for dealing with all of them are the same. Whether raw or cooked, you need to know how to shell them and how to remove the dark intestinal vein.

PREPARING PRAWNS

Most large prawns have a black intestinal vein running along their backs. This is unsightly, and its gritty texture is unpleasant to eat, so it should be removed. If you buy raw prawns, remove these veins before cooking.

3 Remove the dark intestinal vein with the tip of the knife. Discard the vein. Rinse and pat dry with paper towels.

1 Peel off the shell, being careful to keep the prawn intact and leave no flesh on the shell. All the shell can be removed, including the tail end, or you can leave the shell on the tail for an alternative presentation.

2 Make a shallow cut along the back of the prawn with a small knife, to expose the dark vein. Carefully loosen any overhanging membrane that may tether the vein to the prawn.

CRAYFISH

Although crayfish resemble tiny lobsters, they are in fact prepared and cooked in a similar way to prawns. The intestinal vein is best removed before cooking. Twist the centre section of the tail, then pull it away from the body – the vein will come away too.

TRICK OF THE TRADE

KEEPING PRAWNS STRAIGHT
Oriental chefs use this simple technique to prevent prawns from curling during cooking.

Before cooking, insert a long wooden cocktail stick through the centre of each prawn. Remove the sticks before serving.

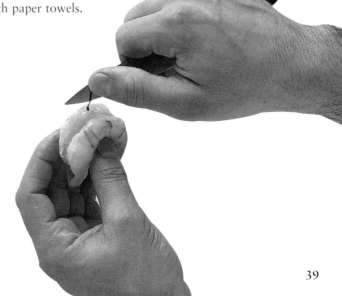

MUSSELS

Choose undamaged, fresh-smelling mussels. Avoid those that feel heavy – they may be full of sand – or light and loose when shaken – they are probably dead. Ensure all are tightly closed; reject any that do not shut when tapped.

MOULES A LA MARINIERE

25 g butter
2 shallots, chopped
2 garlic cloves, chopped
200 ml dry white wine
1 tbsp chopped fresh parsley, plus extra for garnishing
450 g live mussels, cleaned
Salt and freshly ground pepper

Melt the butter in a large, deep pan and sauté the shallots and garlic for 5 minutes or until soft. Add the wine and parsley, bring to a simmer, then add the mussels. Cover the pan tightly and steam for 6 minutes or until the mussels open. Discard any that remain closed. Lift out the mussels, draining their liquid back into the pan. Strain the liquid to remove any sand; rinse out the pan. Return liquid to pan and boil to reduce; season. Serve with the liquid poured over and garnished with parsley. Serves 4.

CLEANING

About three-quarters of mussels on sale today are cultivated. The rest are harvested from the wild. Mussels filter seawater through their bodies to extract nutrients and may pick up any toxins in the water. Whether cultivated or wild, they must be carefully cleaned before being cooked.

1 Scrape off any barnacles from the outsides of the shells with the back of a small knife.

2 With your thumb against the blade, pull out and detach any hair-like "beards" from the hinges of the shells.

3 Scrub each shell briskly under cold running water with a stiff brush. This will remove any sand and thoroughly clean the mussels before cooking. Discard any mussels with cracked shells and any that do not close when tapped. Place cleaned mussels in a bowl of lightly salted cold water for about 2 hours or until ready to use.

From left to right: New Zealand green-lipped mussel; Young marine mussel; Mature marine mussel

SAFETY FIRST

- Do not collect mussels from the wild unless you are certain the water is not polluted, and never collect them in the summer.
- If possible cook mussels on the day of purchase or picking – keep them in a bowl of lightly salted cold water for 2 hours, fresh water will kill them.
- If shells are muddy, or you want to cook them the next day, soak them overnight in cold water with 1 tbsp flour and 50 g salt.

- Discard mussels that stay open when tapped or are cracked.
- Discard all mussels that do not open when cooked.

STEAMING OPEN

To open mussels, and cook the meat at the same time, they are steamed in a small amount of liquid with flavourings such as shallots, garlic and herbs. You can use water for the liquid, but fish stock or cider will give a better flavour. Another choice is dry white wine, as in the steps here for moules à la marinière *(see recipe, opposite page). Always clean the mussels well.*

1 Clean the mussels (see opposite page), then add to the hot wine mixture.

2 Cover pan and steam the mussels for 6 minutes. Shake the pan occasionally to ensure even cooking.

3 Remove the mussels using a slotted spoon; discard any that are shut. Serve with the strained, reduced liquid.

SERVING ON THE HALF-SHELL

Once opened, the meat of the mussels can be removed from the shells and used in recipes, or left in and served in the shells with a sauce, or topped with herb butter or breadcrumbs mixed with chopped fresh herbs. If they are large mussels, their tough, rubbery rings should be removed (see right).

1 Clean mussels open (see opposite page) and steam them open as above, with liquid and flavourings of your choice. Remove them from the liquid and let cool, then prise them open with your fingers and discard the top shells. Loosen the mussels from the bottom shells.

2 Arrange the half shells on sea salt in a heatproof dish. Top each mussel with ½ tsp pesto or garlic and herb butter, and grill for 2–3 minutes. Garnish with a *concassée* of peeled, deseeded and chopped tomatoes, and basil leaves.

REMOVING THE RUBBERY RING

The rubbery ring that forms a brown edge to the mussel flesh should be removed.

1 Clean mussels and steam them open. Remove them from the cooking liquid and then from their shells.

2 Carefully pull off the rubbery ring that surrounds the flesh with your fingers and discard it.

OYSTERS & CLAMS

Both oysters and clams can be eaten raw, or removed from their shells and simmered in soups and stews, baked, or deep-fried. Left on their half shells, they can be topped with a sauce or stuffing and grilled.

OPENING CLAMS

There are many varieties of clam, from the small ones called vongole *in Italy, which can be steamed open like mussels (see page 41), to the larger* palourdes, *or Venus clams, and the huge hard clams or* quahogs *essential to American clambakes and chowders. Scrub all clams well before opening to remove grit and sand, and discard any open or damaged ones.*

1 Hold the clam firmly and insert the knife blade between the shells. Twist the knife to prise open the shells and sever the hinge muscle.

2 With a spoon, loosen the muscle in the bottom shell. If serving clams without their shells, tip both the meat and juices into a bowl.

SHUCKING OYSTERS

Oysters are usually eaten raw and should be opened (or shucked) only just before eating. Discard open or damaged ones. Scrub the shells well before opening.

1 Using a cloth, hold the oyster, rounded-side down, in your hand. Insert the shucker just below the hinge.

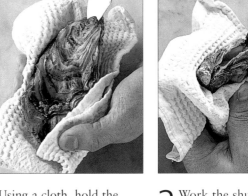

2 Work the shucker further between the two shells. Twist the shucker to separate the shells.

3 Carefully scrape the oyster from the top shell, cut the muscle and remove the top shell. Detach the oyster from the muscle underneath the meat on the bottom shell. Serve on the half-shell on a bed of crushed ice with lemon halves for squeezing. Garnish with blanched samphire, if you like.

SCALLOPS & WHELKS

Scallops can be bought on the shell or ready cleaned and shucked. They do not have to be live when cooked, but they should be very fresh and sweet smelling. So too should whelks, although they are not eaten raw.

OPENING AND PREPARING SCALLOPS

In Europe, shelled scallops are available with their orange roe (coral) intact; in the United States this is usually absent. Scallops on the shell must be opened and trimmed before cooking. To open scallops, split them with a shucker as shown here, or with a small knife.

1 Hold the scallop with its rounded side down in the palm of your hand. Insert an oyster shucker (see opposite page) between the shells close to the hinge.

2 Work the shucker further between the shells. Twist the shucker to separate the shells. Cut the scallop from the flat top shell by scraping it with the shucker.

PILGRIM SCALLOPS

Fan-shaped scallops are also called pilgrim scallops or *coquilles Saint-Jacques* in French. This is because the shell is the badge of the pilgrims who worship at the shrine of Saint Jacques, patron saint of Spain; the badge is always pinned to their wide-brimmed hat. Pilgrims travel through France to Santiago de Compostela in northern Spain, where legend has it that the saint is buried.

WHELKS

These must be cooked in their shells because their meat is difficult to extract while they are still alive. Bring a pan of court bouillon (see page 24) to the boil and add the whelks. Simmer until they are firm but tender.

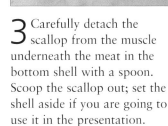

3 Carefully detach the scallop from the muscle underneath the meat in the bottom shell with a spoon. Scoop the scallop out; set the shell aside if you are going to use it in the presentation.

4 Pull away the dark organs from the white adductor muscle and the orange coral with your fingers. Discard the dark organs; rinse scallop under cold running water.

5 Pull off and discard the crescent-shaped muscle on the side of the scallop. The scallop may be cooked with or without the coral. If using the shells for serving, scrub and boil them for 5 minutes.

Lift the whelks out of the pan with a slotted spoon. Remove the whelk from the shell with a fork. Clean the whelk if there is any sign of sand.

SQUID

With a sweet flavour and pleasantly firm bite, squid has long been prized in coastal cuisines. The following techniques prepare squid for numerous dishes, including pasta, stir-fries and seafood salads.

PREPARING

When cleaning whole squid, you need to deal with all of its parts. The pouch, fins, tentacles and ink are all edible; the rest should be discarded. In addition to being used in soups and fish stews, the various parts of the squid can be stir-fried, deep-fried, poached, grilled and even eaten raw in Japanese sushi.

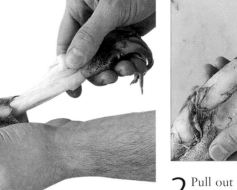

1 Hold the body firmly in one hand and pull off the head and tentacles. Drain the ink and set it aside if you are going to use it in cooking (see box, below).

2 Pull out the "pen", which looks like a long piece of clear plastic, and discard.

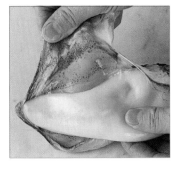

3 Peel off all of the purple skin covering the body (pouch) and the fins; discard the skin.

4 Remove the fins from the pouch with a chef's knife and reserve. Cut the tentacles from the head and reserve.

5 Squeeze the tentacles to remove the beak; cut off and discard. Cut off eyes and mouth; discard.

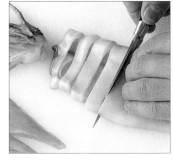

6 After cleaning, cut the pouch into rings or leave it whole for stuffing. Chop the fins and tentacles.

SQUID INK

Black ink is contained in a sac inside the squid. If the sac doesn't break during cleaning, remove it, pierce it and reserve the ink. Sacs can also be bought separately from fishmongers.

In Italy, squid ink is used to colour and flavour pasta; in Catalonia it is used with rice, especially paella. The Spanish dish *calamares en su tinta* is squid cooked in its own ink.

STUFFING

When left whole, the pouch, or body, of the squid makes a perfect natural container for stuffing. Leave a little room at the top because the stuffing swells during cooking. Use the chopped tentacles in the filling, along with other full-flavoured ingredients. A popular Spanish stuffing includes ham, onions and breadcrumbs. A Middle Eastern mixture of couscous, sausage, red pepper and mint makes a delicious alternative.

1 Hold the pouch in one hand. Pipe or spoon the stuffing into the pouch with a large tube.

2 Secure openings with wooden cocktail sticks or sew closed with a trussing needle and string.

PUREED FISH SOUP

Puréeing ingredients that have been cooked in stock and then enriching the purée with cream is a simple method of making soup. The most famous puréed fish soup is the *bisque*, a velvety smooth purée of shellfish.

CRAB BISQUE

A bisque is traditionally made with lobster; however, the same technique can also be used with crab.

1 Soften chopped carrot, onion, potato and celery in butter in a heavy-based pan. Add about 12 small crabs and stir over a moderate heat until deep brown.

2 Flambé a few spoonfuls of brandy and pour over the crab, then sprinkle in 2 tbsp plain flour and stir for 1–2 minutes until the flour has mixed completely with the liquid.

3 Add 2 litres fish stock, 150 ml dry white wine, 2 tbsp tomato purée, 1 bouquet garni and seasonings to taste. Cover and simmer for 45 minutes.

4 Discard the bouquet garni and work the mixture in a food processor.

5 Transfer the mixture to a very fine sieve (a conical one is best) and press through with ladle. Reheat and enrich with cream (see box, above right).

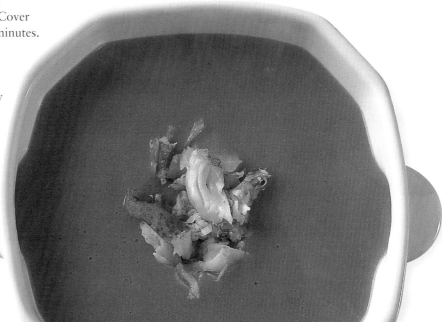

ENRICHING SOUPS

The taste and texture of puréed soups can be enriched with creams and yogurt. Stir them in at the last minute to prevent curdling.

CREAM: Use double cream or other dairy products such as crème fraîche and sour cream. Their high-fat content keeps them stable when heated. They add both richness and an attractive gloss.

YOGURT: As it has a more fragile composition than cream, yogurt and low-fat dairy products should never be allowed to boil or they may curdle.

EGG YOLK LIAISON: This mixture of egg yolks and double cream must be tempered with a little hot soup before it is stirred into the soup – this prevents the yolks from scrambling. Use 2 egg yolks and 1 tbsp double cream to enrich 1 litre soup.

MEASUREMENT CHARTS

Accurate measurements are crucial to the success of any dish. The following charts give quick and easy reference for gauging oven temperatures and converting metric and imperial units for ingredients and equipment.

OVEN TEMPERATURES

CELSIUS	FAHRENHEIT	GAS	DESCRIPTION
110°C	225°F	¼	Cool
120°C	250°F	½	Cool
140°C	275°F	1	Very low
150°C	300°F	2	Very low
160°C	325°F	3	Low
170°C	325°F	3	Moderate
180°C	350°F	4	Moderate
190°C	375°F	5	Moderately hot
200°C	400°F	6	Hot
220°C	425°F	7	Hot
230°C	450°F	8	Very hot

US CUPS

CUPS	METRIC
¼ cup	60 ml
⅓ cup	70 ml
½ cup	125 ml
⅔ cup	150 ml
¾ cup	175 ml
1 cup	250 ml
1½ cups	375 ml
2 cups	500 ml
3 cups	750 ml
4 cups	1 litre
6 cups	1.5 litres

SPOONS

METRIC	IMPERIAL
1.25 ml	¼ tsp
2.5 ml	½ tsp
5 ml	1 tsp
10 ml	2 tsp
15 ml	3 tsp/1 tbsp
30 ml	2 tbsp
45 ml	3 tbsp
60 ml	4 tbsp
75 ml	5 tbsp
90 ml	6 tbsp

VOLUME

METRIC	IMPERIAL	METRIC	IMPERIAL	METRIC	IMPERIAL
25 ml	1 fl oz	300 ml	10 fl oz/½ pint	1 litre	1¾ pints
50 ml	2 fl oz	350 ml	12 fl oz	1.2 litres	2 pints
75 ml	2½ fl oz	400 ml	14 fl oz	1.3 litres	2¼ pints
100 ml	3½ fl oz	425 ml	15 fl oz/¾ pint	1.4 litres	2½ pints
125 ml	4 fl oz	450 ml	16 fl oz	1.5 litres	2¾ pints
150 ml	5 fl oz/¼ pint	500 ml	18 fl oz	1.7 litres	3 pints
175 ml	6 fl oz	568 ml	20 fl oz/1 pint	2 litres	3½ pints
200 ml	7 fl oz/⅓ pint	600 ml	1 pint milk	2.5 litres	4½ pints
225 ml	8 fl oz	700 ml	1¼ pints	2.8 litres	5 pints
250 ml	9 fl oz	850 ml	1½ pints	3 litres	5¼ pints

WEIGHT

METRIC	IMPERIAL	METRIC	IMPERIAL
5 g	⅛ oz	325 g	11½ oz
10 g	¼ oz	350 g	12 oz
15 g	½ oz	375 g	13 oz
20 g	¾ oz	400 g	14 oz
25 g	1 oz	425 g	15 oz
35 g	1¼ oz	450 g	1 lb
40 g	1½ oz	500 g	1 lb 2 oz
50 g	1¾ oz	550 g	1 lb 4 oz
55 g	2 oz	600 g	1 lb 5 oz
60 g	2¼ oz	650 g	1 lb 7 oz
70 g	2½ oz	700 g	1 lb 9 oz
75 g	2¾ oz	750 g	1 lb 10 oz
85 g	3 oz	800 g	1 lb 12 oz
90 g	3¼ oz	850 g	1 lb 14 oz
100 g	3½ oz	900 g	2 lb
115 g	4 oz	950 g	2 lb 2 oz
125 g	4½ oz	1 kg	2 lb 4 oz
140 g	5 oz	1.25 kg	2 lb 12 oz
150 g	5½ oz	1.3 kg	3 lb
175 g	6 oz	1.5 kg	3 lb 5 oz
200 g	7 oz	1.6 kg	3 lb 8 oz
225 g	8 oz	1.8 kg	4 lb
250 g	9 oz	2 kg	4 lb 8 oz
275 g	9¾ oz	2.25 kg	5 lb
280 g	10 oz	2.5 kg	5 lb 8 oz
300 g	10½ oz	2.7 kg	6 lb
315 g	11 oz	3 kg	6 lb 8 oz

LINEAR MEASUREMENTS

METRIC	IMPERIAL	METRIC	IMPERIAL
2 mm	1/16 in	17 cm	6½ in
3 mm	⅛ in	18 cm	7 in
5 mm	¼ in	19 cm	7½ in
8 mm	⅜ in	20 cm	8 in
10 mm/1 cm	½ in	22 cm	8½ in
1.5 cm	⅝ in	23 cm	9 in
2 cm	¾ in	24 cm	9½ in
2.5 cm	1 in	25 cm	10 in
3 cm	1¼ in	26 cm	10½ in
4 cm	1½ in	27 cm	10¾ in
4.5 cm	1¾ in	28 cm	11 in
5 cm	2 in	29 cm	11½ in
5.5 cm	2¼ in	30 cm	12 in
6 cm	2½ in	31 cm	12½ in
7 cm	2¾ in	33 cm	13 in
7.5 cm	3 in	34 cm	13½ in
8 cm	3¼ in	35 cm	14 in
9 cm	3½ in	37 cm	14½ in
9.5 cm	3¾ in	38 cm	15 in
10 cm	4 in	39 cm	15½ in
11 cm	4¼ in	40 cm	16 in
12 cm	4½ in	42 cm	16½ in
12.5 cm	4¾ in	43 cm	17 in
13 cm	5 in	44 cm	17½ in
14 cm	5½ in	46 cm	18 in
15 cm	6 in	48 cm	19 in
16 cm	6¼ in	50 cm	20 in

INDEX